Imitating *Nature*

From Spider Webs to Man-Made Silk

Other books in this series include:

From Barbs on a Weed to Velcro
From Bat Sonar to Canes for the Blind
From Bug Legs to Walking Robots
From Penguin Wings to Boat Flippers

Imitating *Nature*

From Spider Webs to Man-Made Silk

Toney Allman

KIDHAVEN PRESS
An imprint of Thomson Gale, a part of The Thomson Corporation

THOMSON
GALE™

Detroit • New York • San Francisco • San Diego • New Haven, Conn. • Waterville, Maine • London • Munich

THOMSON

GALE

™

For more information, contact
KidHaven Press
27500 Drake Rd.
Farmington Hills, MI 48331-3535
Or you can visit our Internet site at http://www.gale.com

LIBRARY OF CONGRESS CATALOGING-IN-PUBLICATION DATA

Allman, Toney.
  From spider webs to man-made-silk / by Toney Allman.
    p. cm. — (Imitating nature)
  Includes bibliographical references and index.
  ISBN 0-7377-3124-9 (hard cover : alk. paper)
  1. Orb weavers—Juvenile literature. 2. Silk spinning—Juvenile literature. I. Title. II. Series.
  QL458.42.A7A44 2005
  595.4'4—dc22   2004027930

Printed in The United States of America

Contents

CHAPTER 1

The Silk Spinners

Orb weaver spiders have a talent people envy. They can make silk. An ounce (28g) of orb weaver silk is five times stronger than an ounce of steel. It is tougher than the material used to make bulletproof vests. Yet it is also lighter and stretchier than any man-made material. People have tried to collect spider silk for their own use, but their efforts have failed. Spiders are too aggressive toward one another to be raised on spider farms. Crowded together, they would end up eating each other. Spiders cannot make enough silk, either. Five thousand spiders can produce only enough silk to make one dress.

Still, people yearned to take advantage of the amazing properties of spider silk to make strong, flexible material for human use. So some scientists decided to learn how spiders make silk and to try to imitate the process. They focused on the golden orb weaver because it spins the toughest silk of any spider.

An orb weaver spider puts the finishing touches on its web of silk.

Golden Orb Weaver Spiders

Female golden orb weavers are expert web spinners. They live in tropical places like Australia, Africa, and India. From toe to toe, they measure more than 8 inches (20cm) across. They build large wheel-shaped webs that trap insects. The webs can be 6 feet (2m) wide and almost 20 feet (6m) tall. Since the males do not build webs, scientists studied the female orb weavers to learn how nature gave them their special talents.

Glands inside the abdomen of the female golden orb weaver produce strong and sticky silk.

Spinning Silk

The female golden orb weaver makes silk inside her body. In her **abdomen** are six little sacs, called **glands**. Inside these glands is a syrupy fluid called **dope**. Each gland has a different kind of dope. The dope funnels through six tiny tubes, or **spinnerets**. Spinnerets are like water faucets through which liquid dope is squeezed and then ejected at the rear of the spider's abdomen. When the dope hits the air, it instantly dries into a thin strand of silk.

Different glands and spinnerets make different kinds of silk. One kind of silk is used by the orb weaver to wrap up her eggs for protection. Three other kinds are sticky web-building silks that trap insects. Another kind is used for wrapping up insects the spider has caught. The most amazing kind of silk is called dragline silk. The spider uses dragline silk to swing from a tree branch without falling. Dragline silk also is used for the outline and spokes of the wheel-like web. It holds the structure together.

Amazing Dragline

Dragline silk from the golden orb weaver is the strongest material made by any kind of animal. It is so tough that it will not break even if a fat bee flies into it at 20 miles (32km) an hour. Golden orb weavers need dragline silk this strong because, unlike other spiders, they do not build new webs every day.

Fliers Beware!

Many kinds of spiders make webs. Some of these spiders are bigger than the golden orb weaver, but none makes a larger or stronger web. The golden orb weaver's web is strong enough to catch and trap small birds. However, the spider cannot eat birds and does not want to catch such large prey. They make holes in her web. So she leaves dead shells of old insects hanging in her web so that flying birds can see and avoid it.

Dragline Silk in Nature

How the orb weaver spider uses dragline silk to make a web

1 The orb weaver uses tough, nonsticky dragline silk to build the frame of its web. The spider starts by bridging a gap between two sticks.

2 When it has finished building the frame, the spider begins to build the spokes of the wheel-like web. All of the spokes are joined in the center, or hub, of the web.

3 The orb weaver then builds a temporary spiral from the hub to the outside of the web. This temporary spiral will act as a guide when the spider builds the sticky part of the web.

4 After a short rest, the spider begins to build the sticky part of the web. The spider does this by following the temporary spiral from the outside of the web toward the hub. Along the way, the spider removes the temporary spiral by eating it.

Golden orb weavers live in their webs for several years. During that time, they have to repair parts of their webs, but the whole structure hangs together because of dragline silk.

Spider Genes

No one knows how the orb weaver's spinnerets can turn the watery dope from its glands into this fantastic silk. But scientists do know how nature equipped orb weavers to make silk. The ability is coded in their **genes**, inside the cells that make up their bodies. Every living thing carries a blueprint in its genes. Genes are the way living things pass on their characteristics to their babies. Every golden orb weaver carries the genes that tell the spider's body how to spin silk.

By studying the golden orb weaver, scientists have been able to identify the genes used to make spider silk. They have even removed the silk-making genes from the spider's cells. Next, they hope to use these genes to produce silk just as orb weavers do.

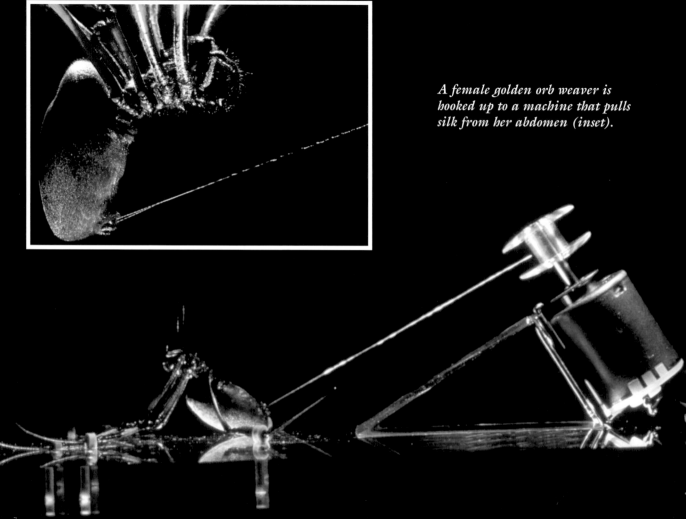

A female golden orb weaver is hooked up to a machine that pulls silk from her abdomen (inset).

CHAPTER 2

Stealing Spider Secrets

Tough dragline silk is the silk scientists want to copy, but imitating the orb weaver's ability to make it was not easy. First, scientists had to identify the genes that make dope. Then scientists had to find a way to use these genes to produce dope. Finally, they had to learn to imitate spinnerets and spin the dope into silk. Dragline production is complicated, but scientists are learning nature's secrets.

Finding Dragline Genes

At the University of Wyoming, a scientist named Randy Lewis spent ten years studying spider genes. He was trying to learn which genes were responsible for making dragline dope. Spiders have thousands of genes. And those genes are so tiny that special microscopes and other devices must be used to study them. After much research, Lewis finally identified two genes that tell spider glands how to make dope.

CHAPTER 2

Stealing Spider Secrets

Tough dragline silk is the silk scientists want to copy, but imitating the orb weaver's ability to make it was not easy. First, scientists had to identify the genes that make dope. Then scientists had to find a way to use these genes to produce dope. Finally, they had to learn to imitate spinnerets and spin the dope into silk. Dragline production is complicated, but scientists are learning nature's secrets.

Finding Dragline Genes

At the University of Wyoming, a scientist named Randy Lewis spent ten years studying spider genes. He was trying to learn which genes were responsible for making dragline dope. Spiders have thousands of genes. And those genes are so tiny that special microscopes and other devices must be used to study them. After much research, Lewis finally identified two genes that tell spider glands how to make dope.

Stealing Spider Secrets

Silkworm Silk

Spiders are not the only creatures that make silk. Silkworms have been farmed for thousands of years for their silk. Silkworm silk is easy to collect, soft to the touch, and readily woven into beautiful cloth, but silkworm silk is nowhere near as strong and tough as spider silk.

Silkworms produce silk that is several times weaker than spider silk.

In 1998 Jeffrey Turner, a Canadian scientist, learned of Lewis's success. He hoped to use spider genes to manufacture dragline silk and asked Lewis for help. The two scientists knew that spider dope glands are similar to **mammary glands**. Mammary glands are the glands in mammals that make milk for their babies to drink.

Turner and some other scientists thought maybe they could use mammary glands to produce spider silk.

Growing Spider-Goats

The scientists chose goats for their experiments because goats are small, are easy to care for, and produce a lot of milk. First, scientists removed **fertilized** eggs from the **wombs** of pregnant goats. In the laboratory, they inserted one dope gland gene into each fertilized egg, adding it to the string of goat genes that form the milk glands. Then the scientists put the eggs back into the goats.

Inside the mothers' wombs, the eggs grew into baby goats. Not all the eggs grew, but in 2001 two baby male goats were born carrying spider genes. They are named Webster and Pete. They look and act just like other goats, but Webster and Pete carry the genes that tell

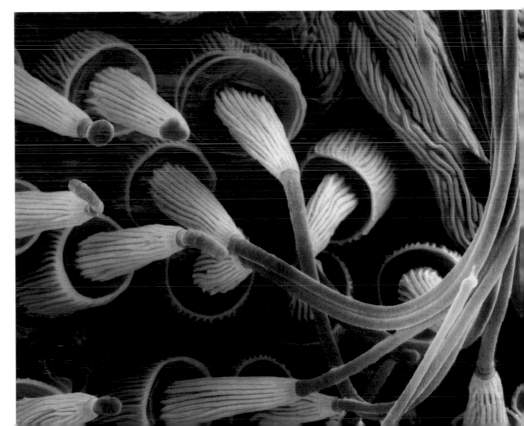

This magnified image shows the spinnerets inside a spiny backed spider as they pump out strands of silk.

mammary glands to make spider dope for dragline silk. When Webster and Pete grew up, they mated with female goats. The genes for making spider dope were passed on to their babies.

Soon, a small herd of goats carried these spider genes. When Webster's and Pete's offspring grew up, the daughters were milked, and their milk was carefully collected. Mixed with the milk was dragline dope.

Making Milk Silk

The scientists separated the milk from the dope. Once they had pure dragline dope, they had to find a way to mimic orb weaver spinnerets. This part of the job was hard. They used instruments like syringes. When the scientists squeezed the liquid dope through the special syringes, out came very thin threads of dry fiber. Dope from goat milk had been turned into spiderlike silk.

Today, scientists continue to make silk from goat milk, although the goats still make much more milk than dope. Each quart (liter) of milk from the goats has only about a half ounce (14g) of dope that can be made into silk.

From Spider Webs to Man-Made Silk

Manufacturing Dragline Silk
How scientists use goats to produce dragline silk

1 Scientists remove a special silk gene from the golden orb weaver spider. The gene is responsible for the spider's super strong dragline silk.

2 Scientists add the gene to a fertilized goat egg, then implant the egg in an adult female goat.

3 The female gives birth to a baby goat that carries the special silk gene.

6 The super strong fibers may one day be used to make automobile seat belts, surgical thread, or bulletproof clothing for soldiers (left).

5 Scientists separate the special silk from the milk and use it to produce super strong silk fibers.

4 When the goat grows up, she produces special silk milk.

Precious Goats

Webster and Pete are part of a breed of dwarf goats from West Africa. These dwarf goats are small and grow to adulthood quickly. Webster and Pete grew up in only about fifteen weeks. Because they and the other goats in the herd are small, they are easy to care for. Because they grow up fast and are able to mate early, the herd can grow bigger sooner.

Scientists discovered the mammary glands of dwarf goats like these could be used to produce spider silk.

Not Perfect, but Pretty Good

Because scientists also do not know how to perfectly imitate spider spinnerets, the goat milk silk is not yet as good as a spider's dragline. It is thinner than a human hair, but not as thin as an orb weaver's silk. Scientists do not know why but the thinner dragline silk is stronger than the thicker silk. The goat milk silk is not as strong as real orb weaver dragline, but it looks and feels like spider silk. And even though it is less than half the strength of dragline, the silk is three times as tough as other man-made materials. It is also stretchy and flexible.

Scientists have figured out how to imitate spider silk using spider genes. In the future, they hope to use their silk-making secrets to develop new inventions that will help people everywhere.

In the Laboratory

To collect orb weaver genes, scientists freeze the spiders in liquid nitrogen. Then the spider bodies are ground up into a fine brown powder. Every cell in the spiders' bodies carries the dope-making genes. These genes are extracted from the powder and are pushed into goat eggs with a very thin glass pipette, or tube.

Goat-milk silk might be used to make sutures that are finer than those used on this patient's injured eye (close-up, inset).

Uses for Milk Silk

Someday, goat milk silk may have many different uses. At present, making a lot of silk is still difficult. The process is very expensive and needs huge amounts of milk. So scientists are working on a variety of projects. Some of these may not succeed while others may eventually become a part of everyday life.

Stitches with Milk Silk

One idea is to develop microscopic fibers for **suture** material for doctors and hospitals. Sutures are the stitches doctors make with surgical thread to sew up injuries or close up the body after surgery. Sutures from man-made spider silk will be much thinner and finer than the sutures in use today. They will be perfect for tying microscopic knots that will not leave scars. Surgeons will use this extra-fine thread for very delicate operations on eyes or on nerves in the human body. Eventually, spider silk sutures may be made in larger sizes for any kind of injury.

Spider Bandages

During the American Civil War, injured soldiers often collected spider webs and used them to bandage battle wounds. Spider silk has been used in medicine for a long time, but there are not enough spider webs in the woods for modern medical use.

A surgeon prepares to use nylon thread to suture a wound. Spider silk may one day replace man-made materials in sutures.

Silk will be very safe to use in people's bodies, too. Human bodies sometimes reject man-made sutures, such as nylon, especially in the eyes or nervous system. The body's protection system reacts as if artificial materials are a danger and tries to get rid of them. Experiments have shown that the body does not reject spider silk.

Spider silk is also **biodegradable**. Some suture material today is biodegradable, but these sutures cannot be used for all operations. Spider silk sutures will be strong enough for any kind of surgery. They will dissolve naturally in the body and will never have to be removed after a wound has healed.

Milk Silk Fishing Lines

In the future, biodegradable silk may have other uses, too. Some of these uses could help the environment as well as people. Fishing line, for example, is now made of nylon. Nylon does not biodegrade. When it is lost or thrown away in the water or on the beach, fish and birds often get tangled in it. Many animals die.

Fishing line made of spider silk would biodegrade over time when exposed to the weather. It would reduce the risk to animals. Earth's environment

Nylon fishing line like this is dangerous to wildlife because it does not biodegrade.

23

would benefit from the use of spider-silk fishing line.

Protecting Soldiers

The U.S. Army is very interested in the strength and lightness of man-made spider silk. The army thinks it can be used to help protect its soldiers. Soldiers on dangerous assignments wear bulletproof vests made from a man-made material called Kevlar. Each vest is very hot and weighs 16 pounds

A Dash of Spider

Webster and Pete are called transgenic goats, meaning they carry genes from another animal inside their bodies. But they are not truly spider-goats. Each transgenic goat is only $1/70{,}000$ spider because each has only one spider gene mingled with thousands of goat genes.

Spider silk might be used to make futuristic full-body armor (opposite page) and lightweight, bulletproof uniforms for soldiers.

Super Strength

A strand of dragline silk is just one-tenth as wide as a human hair, but strands woven together in a rope only as thick as a pencil would make a rope so strong that it could stop a Boeing 747 in midflight.

Light and strong, spider silk has many uses that scientists are just beginning to discover.

(7kg). Moreover, not all high-speed bullets are stopped by Kevlar. Studies by scientists show that a vest made of spider silk would be 20 percent lighter than Kevlar and yet 3 times tougher. Such vests could save many soldiers' lives.

Bulletproof vests will be difficult to manufacture, though. Thousands of goats would be needed to produce enough silk to make bulletproof vests. Each vest would require the milk from 200 goats. So far, there is only one herd of spider-goats, and it numbers about 50. Over the next few years, however, as the goat herd grows, spider silk vests, as well as many other products, could become a reality.

From Spider Webs to Man-Made Silk

The Future of Milk Silk

Someday, spider silk from goat milk may make extremely strong ropes and even cables that can catch fighter jets as they land on aircraft carriers. Because the silk is so light and strong, it may eventually be used to make body parts for jets or racing cars. Seatbelts and airbags could be made of spider silk.

Scientists still have more to learn before spider silk can be used in everyday life. However, thanks to Webster and Pete, milk silk inspired by spider webs may help people of the future stay safe and healthy as well as protect the environment.

Glossary

abdomen: The lower part or back portion of the spider's body.

biodegradable: Able to decay in the environment naturally and harmlessly.

dope: The watery fluid made in a spider's glands that is forced through the spinnerets to become spider silk.

fertilized: An egg that has started to develop because it was joined with a male cell, such as sperm or pollen.

genes: The basic units of inheritance. They code information or provide a blueprint that determines physical traits of people and other living things.

glands: Small, pouchlike organs in the body that produce liquid chemicals.

mammary glands: Organs in breasts or udders that produce milk to feed a baby.

spinnerets: The tiny nozzlelike tubes in a spider's abdomen from which dope is forced out of the rear of the spider's body as a thin strand of silk.

suture: The thread or string that doctors use to make stitches and sew wounds together.

wombs: Organs in female bodies where babies develop before birth.

For Further Exploration

Books

Margery Facklam, *Spiders and Their Web Sites*. New York: Little, Brown, 2001. Readers will learn about spider anatomy and meet several different kinds of spiders. Spiders in this book include crab spiders, fishing spiders, black widow spiders, and more. The golden orb weaver is called the golden silk spider in this book.

Jane Featherstone, *Farming*. Austin, TX: Raintree Steck-Vaughn, 1999. Biotechnology is used with food plants in farming as well as with animals such as goats. Not everyone is comfortable with this interference with nature. A chapter in this book about agriculture is devoted to different ideas about the good and bad parts of moving genes around.

Darlyne A. Murawski, *Spiders and Their Webs*. Hanover, PA: National Geographic Library, 2004. With beautiful color photographs and easy-to-read text, this book describes web-spinning spiders from all over the world. Meet the Hawaiian happy-faced spider, the ogre-faced spider, tiny spiders, and giant spiders. Learn about the many different kinds of spider webs.

Web Sites

Biotechnology Learning Center (www.childrensmuseum.org/biotech/index.htm). Goats and spiders are not the only creatures that have traded genes in the laboratory. Biotechnology is the science of using living things as tools to help people have better lives. The Children's Museum of Indianapolis explains biotechnology research and how it helps people, and the site even provides interesting biotech games.

The Construction of a Wheel Web (www.xs4all.nl/~ednieuw/Spiders/Info/Construction_of_a_web.html). With a series of drawings, this site demonstrates the way a spider builds her web, from the first strand to the finished product.

Spiders (www.rochedalss.eq.edu.au/spider/spider.htm). The fifth-graders at the Rochedale School in Australia have put together a huge Web site with everything anyone could ever want to know about spiders. There are spider facts, spider games, and spider photos. Poisonous spiders, orb weaving spiders, and giant spiders are described. There is even a story about the famous spider-goats.

You and Your Genes (www.niehs.nih.gov/kids/genes/home.htm). Learn all about genes and inheritance on this site from the National Institute of Environmental Health Sciences. Many graphics help to explain the role of genes, DNA, and chromosomes in determining human traits.

From Spider Webs to Man-Made Silk

Index

Picture Credits

About the Author

Toney Allman holds degrees from Ohio State University and the University of Hawaii. She currently lives in Virginia, where she enjoys exploring the woods, hiking, and learning about the natural world.